"The kitchen is the heart of the home"

"The kitchen is a place where you can forget your troubles and just cook"

"The kitchen is a place where memories are homemade and seasoned with love"

"Cooking is love made visible"

"The only thing better than a good meal is sharing it with loved ones"

"The kitchen is where we come together to share good food and good conversation"

"The best memories are made around the kitchen table."

"The kitchen is where we can forget our troubles and create something beautiful"

"The kitchen is a place of comfort, a place where we can be ourselves"

"A messy kitchen is a sign of happiness"

"A recipe has a beginning and an end, but what happens in between is up to you"

"The kitchen is a place
where you can get lost in
the magic of cooking"

"The kitchen is a place
where time slows down
and memories are made"

"The kitchen is a place of comfort, a place where we can be ourselves"

"In the kitchen, as in life, it's the little things that count"

"Good food, good mood"

"The kitchen is where the magic happens"

"Cooking is a form of therapy"

"Cooking is an art form"

"The best memories are made in the kitchen"

"Cooking is a way to show love"

"Food is the ingredient that binds us together"

"The kitchen is where inspiration is born"

"Cooking is a delicious adventure"

"The kitchen is where the joy of life is shared"

"The kitchen is the soul of the home"

"Cooking is the ultimate expression of creativity"

"The kitchen is where dreams become delicious realities"

"The kitchen is where ideas are seasoned with love"

"Cooking is an adventure in every dish"

Made in the USA
Monee, IL
06 February 2024

52977637R00037